SOMETHING WILL COME TO US

Merrilee Cunningham

ANAPHORA LITERARY PRESS

ATLANTA, GEORGIA

ANAPHORA LITERARY PRESS
1803 Treehills Parkway
Stone Mountain, GA 30088
http://anaphoraliterary.com

Book design by Anna Faktorovich, Ph.D.

Cover image: "Child with Dog" by Suzanne Phocas, 1925. Yale University Art Gallery.

Published in 2014 by Anaphora Literary Press

Something Will Come to Us
Merrilee Cunningham—1st edition.

ISBN-13: 978-1-937536-83-1
ISBN-10: 1-937536-83-1

Library of Congress Control Number: 2014949808

SOMETHING WILL COME TO US

MERRILEE CUNNINGHAM

THE MIND'S PLACE

When I imagine in the night
The black is not just night
But something which does not exist
When daytime lends us sight
Then I envision the family of hell
Covers as moths a cloud of deadly night
Which all the day hid away
In a secret shade
And when the morning comes
I feel as if a ship
That flies fair under sail
A hidden rock, escape unaware
That lay in wait,
A mariner, yet half amazed
At perils past, and yet in doubt
As a titanic libido awakes
The sun sleeps
And the light of day
Is often the darkness of desire
Wakening and dreaming life.

MILTONIC DEFIANCE

I would be Abdiel
Flying through a frost of lies
Carried away from all I know
By the great rhetorician's voice.
I am Abdiel, lost to you
And I come home
Through the air as among enemies
As leaves in the wind of an autumn day
Fall, rise, and fall, rolling in the wind.
A thousand, thousand dying leaves
Alone with Satan's hierarchy
The kingdom's god of hell
(doing that Manichean rag)
And that duel of the mind
With hell's black curtained dead
Drawn behind a sleepy avenue
Seen alone at a loud café
I cross the street to meet you unawares
The devil is a hungry hunter
And oh the terrors of the cold
The biddings of the past
Will not subdue the running thought
Escaping out at last:
I am Abdiel swept through hell's gates
Listen and beware the softness of this lovely stare
Fall you archangels, see your home
Float on a burning lake out to sea
Like a whale's red body knifed
By a thousand harpooning machines.
Fall and be damned you devils
In a thousand, thousand eyes
That glue themselves to the passage
Of a clock's ticking, fingered red band

Close your eyes to the beat of our own dead meat
As Abdiel sweeps across the burning skies
Which smoke and belch soot into our lies.
Abdiel, the beloved of God, separates himself
From Satan's red winked pride
Fall you devils down the flaming hole
Of Chaos' long, cremated skies.

WHAT YOU WILL

As you like it,
I, like you, have trained for the role
Of a fool,
A kind of camouflage
Behind my dress, I shoot my wit,
A natural idiot,
I translate fortune into laughter
Lyricist, Satirist, Parodist,
My own extravagance
My own verses
but a parody of me,
A touchstone must be a Jack
So far our to our we ripe and ripe
A thousand profound similes
I make fun of me
As we resemble one another like the book
You look at me and see yourself
Oh that I were just a fool in the forest
And recognize my respondence
Sometime despondence
Pondering
A folly in a mothy coat
A phonograph record of the world of abuse
Hiding the lion until he comes out.

CAT # 1

Today our landlord caught us with a cat
We've had for months but never really thought
That cat could ever so summarily be caught
A bit of life, a wild thing in our rooms,
Bouncing among the chairs,
A Persian cat with long grey hairs,
A tiny prize from out of doors.
Rented rooms rent wombs.

PERDINALES FALLS

Today again I sit on a rock in a dry creek bed
Buzzards glide above my feet,
As I practice swami knots
Binding my lions with external wombs
Of knots to hold me in climbers airs,
The guide runs a factory for adventurers
The bugs make noises, almost words
On a rock wall called smorgasbord
Only the moths do not scream.
Twice now fathers have killed snakes
In front of their sons, water snakes
As women neither cheered nor hissed
But stood by, and watched,
Even the rocks are not safe
From the chisels of time or geologists.
They say the world is getting colder
Do you suppose it's the tom tom beat of hammers
Trying to get their rocks off
But all the rocks turn into dry beds of sand

As the children search the paths
Where creatures can be found.
I think of childless office women
Calming their sterility with house plants
Could there be anything more horrid
Than a philodendron
Cultivated because it cannot die.
The children hold hands
Talking softly of Indians, hills, and war,
I wear deer skin moccasins with beads
And will never put on turquoise again
For I cannot find squash blossoms here
Except in the children talking
Below the roar of van engines.
The lizards run like chickens
Grasshoppers must be very strong.
And hummingbirds very small.

PICARA, PICARA

I am not Becky Sharpe,
Though I labor to understand her
The anti-heroine
I didn't want to be
Nor Amelia
I am just half Becky Sharpe,
The daughter of Becky
As mother sent me to charm school
Run by whores the Atlanta Journal said
But I have needed the con-woman
Sharp-dealing
My naiveté
Picara, picara
Vanity Fair
My children would have starved
Without you.

SLEEPING WITH DOGS

I used to love my life
Consider myself happy
But now I only like
Sleeping with Meredith's dogs
I only trust the dogs
To tell me that they want my company
Turning back
To my old dog self
Do I care what the dogs think?
Do they know how much I love
Their company.
I have become what I refused so long to be
Animal woman, pathetic animal woman
No better than the old lady with hidden cats.

SELF-STRANDING

Sometimes the pine trees do not remind me of Georgia
But of Chinese calligraphists who I have never met.
The swamp hen rarely visits
As I sit in a foreign city and wait for
Los Angeles to take it over.
I am in Houston and so is he
And we sit untogether.
I left the pine trees
Because the needles hurt my skin?
And eyes.
I have built a house so far

From anything I care about
That I can't live here.
My urge to build
Always eventually conquers
My urge to tear down.
Is that still virtue?
Or like everything, just another need
Showing its ugly head
The pine trees are still here and there
Whispering in the dark.
I miss them even when I teach
Strangers I have known less than a decade.
Who is taking flying lessons now?

THE CITY OF DIS

I see this winter the wildwood,
A vision of dry dying,
And only the naked-necked trees,
And only the children knew,
As I walked the paths of a whirling wood
As a hat seeks the center, stopping to rest,
After running ravaging through this dark day.

The sparrows summon me to a little circle,
Where they flew around in a merry dance,
And they dug their claws in the flesh of trees,
But the trees which swayed their bobbing heads,
Said yes, side to side,
Then no, back and forth,
They mean nothing, but what bark and needles of pine
Can mean.

The wind pecked at me, not hungry for warmth,
But pushing me to hurry, then changing its mind,
And sending me back tumbling toward meadows,
Toward the City of Dis.

I have come from the burning black land,
With its stone walls cut in measured rock,
Which scrapes against the skin, like steel grey
Scrapes the sky.
I have come from the City of Dis,
Where the air stole my breath,
As it rushed by, like a late shopper,
Or a shop girl hurrying towards shop walls.
Let us go, just two, through the walls and woods,
Walk the pine straw paths,
 Intruders out of the land of Dis,
Out of the land of dry doom.
Let us go, you with your book,
And me with my pen in my hand,
To a soft green land,
I call, so come,
For the owl calls, calls the poor.
The poor, of the City of dis.

The Lark:

I have watched you walk from the steel grey way,
To the linnet's home in the answering pine.
You turned the sparrows' circle as the wind turns,
You walked the pine needle path as the wind walks,
Man's the hunter, searching this wood,
Who has come from the grey land of Dis,

But for years before time, before the pines,
Before the slenderly great.
Though not before the weird-faced oaks.
You have not turned to the sparrow circle,
As snail horns creep across the basil leaves,
Or walked the path of the wind, the nodding of pines,
Only the half-breeds remember the days,
When you were a traveler still.
Only the brown beaver remembers the Mays,
When you turned the right ways, and came,
Came from the houses of almighty Dis.

The Thrush Castle:

We wandered far from the pine needle path,
Far   from the grey smoking land behind,
Till you and I and   your voiceless son,
And the linnets there in the tenderest tree,
Were all the company we had here,
Were all the living things that we could see.
Then the mute boy saw the tiny home,
Of the brown thrush-king who sang the mute boy's song,
 And the song was all that we could see,
For the music danced in a fairy lad,
And those green notes were all that we need be.

Gone is the thrush castle,
gone the green wood.
And the mute boy, he too is lost.
And we lie here, in the City of Dis.
Here in the grey smoking burn.
And all that we can hear is a steel grey sea,
But you might still on this steel grey day
Sing a song from the pine needle path,
A song of the thrush-king's home
And the green notes we used to be.

THE HOUSTON AIRPORT TRAIN

Mother and Julie are neither place
Lin's in Terminal A
For they
Were on their way on one side
I'm on the other
Or are Mother and Julie in between
The Houston airport train
Closed the door
"Goodbye Baby"
Separating you from a sister
Not by time, but by place
Time, not place
Time-place.
The door is closed by a machine
You cannot see
I'm part of you,
Apart again
I sit here waiting at Terminal B
Lin's at Terminal A
Sharon asks no coins as they arrive
To be with me in B.

COAL MINES

I am red meat

You are little better;
Waiting to be red meat
For the sun.
Stench and flies in the afternoon
Smell and feel an afternoon tune.
The nose and other pits
We mine;
Flash our miner's lights
Into night hollows.
Flies in a long black placenta
Near the meat-eating sun…
Ash, ash, blazing coal
You poke and stir;
Shovel a gaping sore
In a thin grey film of death glitter.
We carry black pails,
 little lunch coffins
And spread our debris,
While we breathe soup
In mother's privates parts.

SOMETHING WILL COME TO US

I had hoped to be the Strategist
Cassio taking Iago's place at last
Helping my loved ones
Get better
But I am nothing more than
The fool, not even
The Great Tactician
Despite all my years at schools
The learning of many rules
I am no mistress of land ways
Nor can I breathe in sea water
I have not blinded a god's child
But another desperate problem
Lies, surprisingly,
on my family's horizon
Over and over again
Something will come to us.

ON REREADING AN OLD BOYFRIEND'S LETTER

Maybe I have had more love than I deserved,
So why complain about the lonely days and nights
I spend now.
Maybe this is what I have earned
With the way that I treated you.
Maybe I need to learn to sit quietly
Alone, and think about
What I have done.
Just as my mother suggested
So long ago.
Maybe this is the only way that I can avoid
Triple Nemesis
Rearing her ugly heads.

THE UNIVERSITY DEPARTMENT OF ENGLISH IN SOUTH TEXAS

There is no denying that we work hard
Though the halls seem abandoned
Much of the time;
Students searching, searching
Patchy, patchy
Or that we do a lot of pretending
(we are trained in pretending)
Shocked, I tell you shocked
That I have published nothing in twenty years
Shocked, I tell you shocked
That more don't complete my course
That my desire for deference
For not giving you a reference
Has caused you to drop my class.
(You haven't been black lately have you?)
Back, black, back, black
Ojala que no.
 Wander about the halls
With the other searching students
Unless a dean can save you
(We keep the deans busy;
Maybe they could give us our own dean)
Or you just give up and go.

Three colleagues in that corner room
Hiding from students
Losing their lives and minds
One piece of research among them
Telling me what I have done wrong.
While Susannah and Meredith
Go to schools fit for lawyers' children
And I think of what I must do
To keep them there.
Like Ben Franklin in London
Before Parliament;
Hours of saying nothing.
I am no professor
Nor do I profess.
I am a mother.
About that they were right.
Confirmed at last.
We are the Department of English
In this huge Texas town
Que pensa sobre estica?

LOUISE MALLOY, LOUISE CALLAWAY, LOUISE WATKINS AND ME

This might have been a last illness
As I grow so thin that the paleness
In my face sends friends far away from my voice
Fearing for their own health
Watching least I might cause a cancer's growth
To form in their wombs or breasts
I cough.
They touch their chests
And feel dust at their lips
Brush it away at the backs of slender-fingered hands
Stroke quickly at their thin-lipped mouths.

Does the hollowness about my eyes mirror them
In a frame they do not like?
Are my attempts at being gay
Only to confound their feelings as they wait
To see me grow pretty again or fade?
Will my very touch destroy you,
For your life's so mean that I can take your strength
Sucked in with a deep desperate breath.

Fool…We were all ill before the cough.
Then you took my words and we kissed
The husbands and loves,
More soft than they could, they called,
As fever caused that rose-blush
 And we grew thin and chic,
Then bold, old and wise.
Now our plumpness mocks this stick,
A switch I balance my mind on.

Have you breathed-in Death
Cocoon worms waiting...
Breathed in before you saw,
The pallor of sick green
Beneath our subtle rouges and creams,
Hidden by silken bandages from Saks.
Silk to hide a festering bloom.
Women without breasts---lost to kill cancer,
Proud scars feed children too
Wombless women, not castrated
On a Sunday afternoon
Dying discreetly so they can
Still be invited
Not over excited
Left un-shut up.
No longer daring to walk too close.
Least their friend fear
A recurrence
Or transference
They hush their death-gasp
In the end so not to offend.

Can they give Death to you?
Then why did they die?
We are slowly cut out, little pieces.
A bit here, another there.
Til only dim dust and a dry clay brain remain.
As we march through a green wood
And melt again into the dark.
We are all growing so thin

Together.

MADNESS #303

The rhythms of the head's beating
Pounding my eyeballs
With the hammer of my ears
Says and will play
Its mad melody
Vibrations from the shrill
In the ear and eye
Turn the neck
To a wobbling spring
As the nerve ends jump out
To save themselves.

ALICE AND
THE QUEEN OF HEARTS

The mind's pattern a clear deck
Of Alice's setting in terror's land
A cat with candle eyes
A hat of some degree
An otter with an oyster out at sea
Some bottled sweets,
A floor, a book of Freud,
A wrist watch hand ticking
Silently behind a door
Like an ogre's grinning red wand,
Pointing the moment as it moves
Big house, little house, Bartholomew's Fair,
Alice goes wondering
What's in a yellow cat's stare?

A PERSIAN RUG

The red wand weaves its toured design
Those distant dynasties of a darkened sphere
Viennese windows, a palace at Agra
The grand azure of scrolled geometry
Hastens to cross the black design
Toward frozen spots of white.
I have taken the truths you once gave me
And woven them into an orderly lie
For as I walk on carpeted green
Dust bellows enshroud the floor
Darling, you have stars in your beard
Impudent molecules of stuffed balconies,
The rug is an orderly   rag
To carpet the cold stone floor.

YET ANOTHER DANCER AND ANOTHER DANCE

A featherless bird walks across the floor
A no-faced girl with lovely arms
In harmony about to soar off to a balcony,
Away from us, the still audience unmoved,
Watching the flight of a sparrow dressed in stars.
Ladies fans move no more in the hall,
Nor do gentlemen get up to smoke
While there on stage we watch like antiquarians.

Dances mean what they are, for dance is old
What does it seem to those up close or far away
Too much rouge, untightened brows
And sweat careening down a powered cheek
But to a gallery, perhaps it's still
A moment in ruined marble passing before a goldsmith's bird
An image of movement, or moment itself
As we murder to dissect.

Unconsciously he moves across the page,
Or painfully remembering lessons past
Challenging the light between dance and darkened hall
Dissolving in tension the movement matter
While we rummage the hall for someone we know
And rattle the ice in a cherry smash
I think of you as I am here, rehearsing a tap dance.

MOTHER'S PILLS AND BOOZE

No slashed wrists
Stomach pumps in white rooms
Just booze and pills and cigarettes
In a chinessiere wing-back chair
No Doctors in white covers
Steel cranks on the bed
Just one attempt after another
To prove she is not dead.
I remember when I was small
And mother would call from the bannister
And in a very clever way
Suggest that today was a new game
For she was reconsidering suicide
Which way best to end it all
And I was the person responsible
For all the things she had not been
Even though she had been enough.
Her game was to nearly hide her suicide
"That's not what I meant at all"
So I could never detect
Just how and where and when
It would end.

MARLOWE'S MELODY

There is no joy in this red-gashed earth
For those who argue with themselves
Too subtly
Over their reasons, doing, being
Seeing too much for safety
Feeling too much for joy
Only gashes and slashes
And glitter of ashes
Marketing the heat
Of our own red meat
We deceive, we deceive
In our own desire to believe
That self instruction
Splendid destruction
Is not our end
To defend
Our enemies
Brutalizing the self
Made monster
As our bodies cry to bone dry brains
Flee!

SPLIT SOUNDS

Everything is breaking
A piece here and there
Time spent waiting
For a conclusion
Aids but dissolution
The attempt to fix in the mind
One single whole
No longer matters
The lie's too old
Then clergy now
Has come at last
But relics of holy fragments have scattered
Everywhere
Rooms find no center
Windows and walls no perimeters
Work has no theme
No simple motif
Music is jammed
Belief is a thief
As an 8 piece bathing suit
In patches
Pasted the excess fabric
 at the knees
Pitiful humans
Afflicted fragment
Too many people
For snatches of space

Wonder who's coming
To take our place
Running backwards
In a cripple's race.
What you remember
Before you lost your head
Is nothing is living
Or really quite dead
The line, the lined walked
Every day
Ways, trails, bridges
Traditions, illusions
Roads to confusion
A lovely allusion
Splatters the way
Runs down the hall
Screams in a room
Mahler, Mahler, Mahler
Make a sound
Repeat a bar
Jar, mar, tar, car, czar…
Far.

JASPER

Those lines that lay about
A jasper jar
Swirl and hurl the red lines at its heart
In a play of red and beige
The life line of stone
Without voice
Cold and caged
In sordid trials
Running about the distended tracks
In polished rock
From a rotten Italian town
Rubbed with fingers of a wheeled man
Polished and shaped
Formed in the filth of smoke stacks
Factorized men
Artists no longer polish stones
A big wheel shapes life
Death, cold stone, dry bone
Suffering red rock bleeds in the white
Of jasper nights.

VERANDA SITTERS

I am the end product
Of a long, long line of great veranda sitters
People who could sit and wait
And never move or ever talk
Until they had
Something to do or say,
Sitting carefully
Less the reeds in the wicker chair
Should finally give
For once we fall
We must get up
or rest less comfortably.
Now never think because I claim
The luxury of rest
It is because of wealth or dignity,
Or all those lies that Georgians have
To explain why they have spent
So many mornings, evenings, afternoons,
Watching folks go by,
Smelling cooking cabbages next door
Or down the street,
It's only because
You see
We never had any place to go
Worth moving
So we sat here for five generations
Til we wore holes in our rockers
Ruts in the floor
And here we sit
And shall sit
Evermore.
La.

MY ODYSSEUS

Return no more you magistrates of holy hell
To the man of trouble
For the black demurring circles of a dying mind
Can hold memory of these
The great archangel of Dante's tomorrow afternoon
Is no pattern of you
As a regenerate man
Replaces the swan wings of light
In a fantasy of you
For a blind poet's only   sight.
Dante, Dante, you had to put
Odysseus, The Great Deceiver in Hell.
Trouble, we have a problem.

MACROSCOPE

I haven't talked to her
Haven't you guessed
I don't often have access
When she's here
I am gone
When I am gone…
Well you know.
And when she's not here
Well. I'm an idiot
Barely able to dress myself
Badly
Oedipa, Oedipa
show up in front of bosses please
flip, flop, flip flop
there she goes
in a class,
never a committee
(She might not like committees)
She shows up when she damn well pleases
Fool, fool,
Mithras, Mithras,
Band of sisters
Wear the cloak

Make me a bridge to her.
"O.K. You're a bridge."

RED ROVER

I, The universal goddess, matrix of destiny
Making my appearance once again,
Ask you to come home.
You have seen me in a multitude of guises
Sumero-Babylonian, the cosmic female
A redneck virgin in the morning star
An evening star, a harlot from Rome, Georgia
Lady of the night sky
The consort of Mars
Why can't I be
Your first wife and your second
Then I'll be all your many wives
As if you were the sheik of Araby
With so many dancing girls
"What' s her name" from "oh, you know,
They're all the same."
Dear Tricksey man, better than
That cross between a shepherd
Ad a border collie
Come home,
I cross borders in my head
and want you here.
I am the youngest thirty-two year old
You'll ever know
And you are thirty-three and twenty-two
Only to me.

A CHRISTMAS GULLYWASHER

We had all eaten before Christmas fruit.
There was a warm, most unDecember rain
Kathy and Fred, grandmother and I
Washed dishes in the kitchen's warm glow
The extended family's breaking up you know.
The South's a lovely place for Christmas
Whether we deserve its joy or not
And if the civil war killed Grandpa Curtis
This moving off has killed us all the more.
The Rain is washing out
The scum under the house
And the dogs are wet and whimpering in the shed
While cars make squishing noises in the street
Our Christmas lights go on and off
And Daddy's tracking in rotten leaves again
From a constant, most unChristmas rain.

SITTING ON A COW

Sit carrots and peppers in chairs made of clay
They cannot lie with one in the wind today
I am dancing, just dancing over their eyes
Through windows of light that play outside the door
Ask me to tell you to see more and more.
 Swing my garden as high as I reach
Above all those handfuls of sky
While feathered ducklings give good mornings, good byes,
Watercress highways have led by my way
Since when the red good book was ready to die
While mullins are getting quite close to my eye
The kin is so calm because I'm alone
But red wanded fireflies dance in my eyes
In a wall of the garden which sleeps in my head
While everything's dancing just above my eyes.
On that day you'll know, but may now wonder
While I listen to the black bird ask me why
All this without is headed within
And the blackbird within is moving without,
I was pulling skies apart as I sat on a cow
But I've looked upon the parching sun
And never begged for water or goodbye
I sat down at the banquet there
And never asked, a child's small share
For I know I've found the mirror
That was missing in my mind
On the other side of time,
Sitting on a cow.

EUPHEMORA 73

I own my own wristwatch and entertain
My curtains and my bedding are my own
Nor is suspect my bath tub
A neat porcelain about the size
Of coffins fully grown.
I measure time in words and just today
Began a sentence in my smaller room
Which lets out the monsters I call my mind
Like half a cockatrice's egg might do
While everyday I pass the rug and walk
To greet the rock-faced postman full of holes
Like covers on a copper warming pan,
A rotten rustic apple soaked in cinnamon
And water, sounded in the nose and always
Carrying messages, carrying messages,
His hair like Uncle Rufus's
Who hung upon his mothy pants
A subject of great mirth in his thin legs
Which wobbled at the knees and laughed
Like apples in a tub
I take walks in summer
Winter, I watch the sun bounce
tomorrow I expect at least
one piece
of junk mail
from the pitted man.
Sundays, they don't bring mail.
I chew gum most of the afternoon
begin a sentence of a letter to you.

IRIS

You have refined eyes my dear
Like tried metal run through green
Steams the mist to entertain
The mariner still out to sea.
We guide the seaman cross the deep
Or make a bridge with battered walls
Which hold Assyrian bones
Scraped into heaps of carcasses
Counted by kin and peers of Asia.
My dear did I ever tell you
You have magnificent eyes.

CHRISTMAS IN GEORGIA

Laying by a lessening Christmas fire
Which gives no heat this morning
Surrounded finally by Georgia
Far around me in this drawn out core
Nodding pines like busy housewives
Sweep the sky, back and forth,
And this living room warms me
Without fire
Because burning eyes see, back and forth
Far away the Marshes of Glynn, which
Cool and warm, cool and warm,
Even the marsh hen
And I whisper "feliz navidad, little hen."

Colder than me in your marsh home
Where all is easily washed away by the sea
A more ruthless housekeeper,
Back and forth, back and forth,
Like out-of-town relatives,
Or sins.
But for now there is a faint glow here
An ember in this last burning log
Which marks, in midtown,
The very center of my mythical state
Which does not exist unless you see
Those pins in an outer circle
Nodding their heads in referential mania,
Back and forth, back and forth,
Unless you hear the catbird's call
And look into his one good eye and see he knows
That any fool could leave this place
And wander through a wood or world.
Is he following something or
Is something chasing him?
Now that I'm home, I've begun to eat
Again.

BEDROOM SLIPPERS

I get a great deal of consolation
Out of my new, blue bedroom slippers
And although I am forced by the cerebrum
To admit the uterine stuff of shoes
Not to mention the added dimension of bedroom
And while their fluff might leave a smile
On knowing lips —a story there,
My feet for even women have them, —
 Retreat into the warmth of yet another womb
Saved from the daily breech
Of high heel tortures, a patent black lie,
And the dream at night of that sit down job
When one could wear, bedroom slippers,
To work.
But how could students pay attention
To ladies without he added dimension
Of six-inch heels.

SICILIAN FEVER

They always whispered those of Sicilian days
"Black is the beauty of the brightest day"
Hercules, here is where you really lived
Pollex and your twin, farming sending food
To Greece or Rome,
Ship him to the girl's school
Then send Achilles to Troy.
A golden ball, the Agrigentine sun
Passed through its fuel of silver waves
He binds his temples now with clouds
And tempers his own lively heat
Waiting a razzle-dazzle Parisienne death.
I walk the angle leached to Syracusa's
Sicilian port walls
Despite the red hot breath of sentinels.
And the threat of Athenians dying in Salt mines
I could stay here.

TRYOUTS ON THE 1963 NORTHWESTERN DEBATE TEAM

A Saturday morning
Fall was in the air, cool,
But I was not
Just fall; just fall
The only girl in a sea of navy blue blazered men
(Was that really true?)
Waiting for a place on the debate team
My flowered dress tasteless in among the properly attired
(Might as well have been made from a flour sack)
No one said I wouldn't get my chance
It was not, for me, their gender
But their blazers
It was their navy against my army of springing flora
On Lake Michigan that morning
And my out-of-season flowers and me,
we ran
Like Cleopatra from Octavius.

I'm not saying that they wouldn't have given me
My place
If I had worn a blazer
But my flowers just sailed through a sea
Of blue
Never having spoken a word
And left the men to themselves
The only girl, like in Physics class,
Left the field
Without uttering a sound
In my spring dress.
Just fall; just fall.

EMILY 2000

Here I go writing to Emily again
Losing her mother to death
Not such a gentleman now, huh
Em
Huh
Huh
How folded up I feel
After the loss of mother…
A champion mother,
Lately companioning me,
And sister
Like your poem
I have put away
Summer clothes in Emily's upstairs drawer

That has to share room
With so many poems
Life before and after our mothers
The great caesura
Running late, running late
So far from me
Meets only at me her
For someone who never leaves dropping in the fall
The youngest and the youngest
Peg, Bell, Marian, and Mom
The women I have loved
Have begun the great
Desertion
For I miss them inside on the outside
And she missed them inside, inside, inside
Visiting them
Only in the smaller upstairs room
Where once I spent five minutes
Running to see Emily
In Amherst
While my family waited in the car
Outside-inside-outside.

ACADEMIC GREED

Will I ever leave
Willy the shake?
Will they have to rip this course
out of my ancient, grasping, boney hands?
Queen Lear, Queen Lear
Are you still here?
I will bow out
Gracefully, next time.
Better than l did before.
When will I stop running toward
Our words
Like tiresome Kent
Or Mad Tom
Unseemly
In an old woman
Greedily
Happy for another date
Before the rest is silence.

SYNECDOCHE

Like Keats, the answers I get from objects
So often depend on the questions
I have asked them, finding them
Instrumental,   a symbol
An image, artifice, Freud's vase
With Oedipus staring down the sphinx
Enigmatic, the connundra, marble muse
Up through the mneumonically synecdochal
Springs a dazzling gradgindery
The eloquent totem
Focused delirium
Products of the society that made them
Recovering archetype seekers
In 12 step programs
Sacrificial
A fence against contemporary atrocities
Sow a fantastic reality
Traveling through objects
But what of the here-we-come age of
High widgetry
Shall we long for our computer on our belt
"O, Steven, I do love you so."
While there are empires of the imagination
Wonder rooms inside.

LESSER GARDENS

A winter afternoon toward twilight
Fresh from no snow blanket,
I feel the poor soggy soil
Cold since Christmas
Dead really.
Winter at last
Except for Irises, Spring gentilians.
No gravel-surfacing for me
Even in lesser gardens
The roots of the plant here
(slugs less willing to crawl
Over stone surfaces)
Find no one to eat
Surely a little gravel
In a muted color of course
Would help life
Happen – my phalanx of bulbs
Stop the dry rot
Meet disaster
A little surface gravel
Can do some good stopping the extremes
Divert the water
So important for gravediggers
As your water is a great corrupter
Of your whoreson or daughter
Excavation
Better for winter flowering
An August
But then one has to beware
Of orphaned seedlings
And then what kind of gardener are you?

CHIT CHATTING WITH FINGERS

Odysseus at my beck and call
That's right
No wonder sometimes
 I seem
Well,
What would he do in this case
I'm hoping soon to stop
Believing that I can
Communicate with objects
Stamp boxes, rings
Particularly rings
Which adorn the finger
As they talk conferring, no doubt,
Necessary information
To succeed in the day.

FREUD'S FUGUE I

We saw this winter the wild wood
A vision of dry dying
And only the children knew
As we walked the paths of a whirling wood
Like a half-wild dog seeking its center
Stopping to rest
After running and ravaging through this dark day.

If only sparrows would summon us to a circle
Where they flowed around us from the gods
Any gods, so many gods to not believe in
The trees said yes, side to side,
Then no, back and forth
They mean nothing but what bark and needles can mean.
Freud. Freud
So cold now.
I have come from the burning black land,
With its stone walls cut in measured rock,
Which scrap again the skin, like steel grey
Scrapes the sky
I have come from the City of Dis
To visit with you.

AN AUTUMN STORM

There is a stormy madness in this night
The wild wind's midwife, autumn birthing winter
Begun nine months before in gentler love
But Spring has fathered such a cruel child
That months will pass before death makes him mild
Through her thunderous pang-cries I sit and write
The he-child knocks to boldly ask me why
I live in a world in small
A quiet room
Protection from the outside world of gloom
A prisoner cloistered in a little tomb
Condemned to live my fatherless lie so bold
While butterflies and sparrows die of cold

Then I'll exclaim, "Get out, you have no right
To enter cottage windows in this night
I own this house, see here I have the deed
You made the storm, live in it then, God speed.
You gave me flowers, those blue and yellow days
Sent kisses with a boy's spring-tendered ways
And you yourself, you winds, caressed me then
You whispered to me close and far away
You held me with your own strong-arms in sway
But you're no bridegroom to demand on sight
A winter's coupling paid by one spring night.
Caliban, Calihan
Where does the storm come from;
Who sent it here?
What or who do you fear?

Don't waste your fire in lightning when you could
Give extra ours of brightness if you would
That self-same clarity
Men would call charity
Sent as a love token against the dark
The white streak so short, so brightly violent
Will never make me love your strength the more
But rather joins my nerves, its miniatures
And tells my brain what foolishness it wrought
To trade one small bronze life for golden night
Is pleasure, even love, so dearly bought
Dear dark haired boy your gentle showers died
And of our greying cold I'll not be bride."

BACKWARDS

I had to wait a long, long time for love
He didn't come to me in tender days
And budding was a gathering of words
And books, pictures, poems, philosophers.
The child was quite as serious as the girl
The woman's much more frivolity
In dotage I'm surely bound to be a roaring fool in a quiet world.

I waited long and almost knew
That love had gone ahead of me
But as I settled for a duller life
The stern grandmother-child in me
Gave up, ran off, and so I loved you.

MY HUSBAND'S HOUSE

Sometimes I look to find a fault,
That I might leave, and so have done our life.
Some wretched lack which would excuse
A relaxation or vacation
A sort, informal fascination
And other times I see in other men
Nobler lives with great stony houses
Rambling roomy, but cold as winter's wake.

Then warmer nights, I bear my newborn Lust
Conceived by darker eyes than your good watery blue
Dash-about men who thunder and shout
Disturbing the old comfortable rooms,
Stirring my venom-blooded heart
So loudly that I slap my breast
In hopes of stopping the grisly tale
Of faithless wenches and harlot's stench.

As I go dusting round my heart,
I find a lot of old sensations
Worn emotions, ready for the pail.
But one thought lingers as I touch the door
To leave the house that's old and falling down.
One mil-dewed phrase creeps from my mind's cellar
And that one thought sends me dusting, painting
Washing Chinese willow cups for tea:
The husband's house I thought to leave is me.

THE FAMILY PARTY

Why must you believe
That everything lovely which sparkles and dances
All that moves so softly
Must be as empty unfeeling as a decorative vase
And all the laughter that we share
Is nothing more than the shadow of emptiness
And all the smiles of summer nights
Are children telling lies out of themselves?
The jokes on myself that I allow
In the security of private friends
Are no longer jokes when told
To glaring strangers in a splendid house
Who hold over me their chandeliers
To see into what I am, and where I might be
Broken like a wishbone for hall mirrors'
Distorting frames
We throw our knives in a public place
Where strangers may see, laugh and gear
Because they no longer have effect
In the privacy of quiet rooms
We have moved a long, long way
When gin and tonic brings out
The garbage's often lidded cans,
Chained against rats
Lit by car lights passing in the night.
We search to find a flow; an easy job
To reveal it discreetly to a clinking room,
Where civilization is reviewed
Over snails and cocktails
And garbage pails in   the light
And the glare shows poor running sores
Made more painful by the unkindness
Of kind friends.

SLEEP

Our stupid rust buys a lot of pleasant dreams
And we do exhaust ourselves
So what wonder we are not
Murdered in our sleep
as bodies lie over muslin sheets
And we return to colder stone.
Only the sleepless believe
That sleep is an enemy
And only the sleepless know
How wonderful his conquest is
As they resign to rest.

Sleep is but a disappearing banquet
And we are empty
Excepting an illusion of rest.
Not even the resolved to resist
Such glimmering fruit.
Yet I am banished from the table
As a naughty child
The unquiet ones never taste
Nor sup at communion table
Without fearing the guilt
Or stealing someone's
death
For a little rest and peace
A whole day's guilt is made

The shine and ooze of muddled lies.

DEBTS

You will become hard and world worn
As the toothless poor that wander in the streets
Below the softness which I still see
In the quiet lines of our half spoilt face
Will devour like wolves husbands and friends
In search of artifice to save off mental rot
 fat sliding slowly bending to decay
And when you are that wet-eyed seamless wench
You will see, as you go old and creaking
Yourself in some soft floating girl
And people will laugh to watch you claim
That she is what you were, half are,
As now you in all our artful loveliness
Fear already that hag is part of you.

Now is the middle
Stranded between two selves
And that land lies between two larger waves
And we are pulled as we do grasp the lines
For no weight anchors such fragility.
You love, are but one small piece of clay
One land of rest between dark waters.
No sea is so terrible through dark and alone

Because you bare some wrinkles, greying hairs
Which should have otherwise first been my own.
To owe that debt and leave unpaid
That ruinous face is crime enough
But not to tell you that I know
That death is dearly bought off once again
As a gull peaks at our cheeks
Hungry for warmth
 as it runs through this bleak day
Searching for a heart that gives up life
Til at last it rests as we three rest
Dark in ravaging the air with starved mouths.

WALKING

Below the proper greetings of the day
The dignified hellos of business friends
A quiet, strained good humor of work a day
And office women walking like movable plants
A world of rape and physicality
Of naked men and shirts tossed over chairs
And if you dare take off your suit coat
You will move into that green world.

The thin-lipped ladies in black and black,
Carefully cover their honesty
So no one will suspect
Sagging bosoms drop over a protruding belly
Nor do the bulging men with bosomed chests
Forget the morning of their ties
Flagellating their own bellies with last year's shirt
Strangling themselves in last's year's britches.

THE GARDEN

I watch the plastic flowers fade
In sunless window cells and tenement shelves
Their dying leaves turn yellow yet will not fall
Rose petals wither but remain
To trace no tomb but kitchens and dinettes
Do they remind you of your love?
Should their owners want a boutonniere
To lend its smell to your musky suit
They stand ready, those never alive
Need not fade who have not bloomed
Were never buds who are flowers
Will never flower who remain budding

But oh the green that' s lost
In a bromeliad
And oh the lost of nurturing and placing in the sun
Those which must have much sun
Those who need shade, little water
A loosening of the too hard dirt

Perhaps only ferns need their plants around them
Like biscuits must have other biscuits to cook
And only children are fit to tend the young
Then these our plastic gardens suit us well
Stamped off and pressed together and sold
For cents.

TWO SOLDIERS

Trying to keep warm and awake,
Two soldiers walking on a winter'd day
Passed by a woodpile along their way
"How many wooden logs to make a fire
To warm the folks in Tyre?"
"Twelve logs, one for each hour of cold,
While they sit talking and drinking tea"
Six for the evening before sleep
Abandoning their comforters so warm
And tiptoe on the cold wooden floor
To place a log against the hearth"
"How much will those logs cost?"
Said the soldier to his friend
"We'll have to ask and fill a voucher form
To buy those logs we need to keep us warm."
"And what of matches to kindle wooden sticks?"
"Why that's our job too,
Didn't they tell you?"

ODE TO MOTHER'S CROOKED NOSE

Our crooked nose parades upon your face
A monarch wavering in his place
A throne to set between two sky blue eyes
A cannon on wheels
Christ and the two thieves,
A large destroyer of a perfect you
So never change that nose you so disguise
It saves an old face, and makes it new.
Ceranna, Ceranna, speak to me
In your wise voice
Smart mother,
Mary, the defender of the weak,
Daughter to the blind mother
Passing, passing.

AN ANTIQUE VASE

I found three pieces of an antique vase
Which once was buried in a hallowed ground
And held ashes of a holy flame.
Now only a red tailless dragon
Moves over the white porcelain
One poor myth-monster
remains to protect what is not here.

It fell. A tension between floor and vase
Shattered the ancient pot.
The very center hit and broke
Or did a quiet wind push it off a mantle
And its contents spilt on wormwood floors
Walked on by Pope or Keats
Swept out like so much dust.

What fierce archangel dropped such a jar
Only to watch it, hear its crumbling noise
What careless domestic refused her glue pot
To such an ancient honorable vase
While mice rushed round it like a gutted oatmeal ben
And a holy cat toyed with the ashes til they proved dead.

Am I, after these long years
To plaster in those many parts
Jagged pieces cannot be recovered
Or uncovered, rediscovered after the lost hours
Of that first day.

All, all thrown away, one by one,
Each at a different moment,
By some wretched fool
Broken in a second.

PREDATOR

Today the cat caught a rabbit
Full of food from the cat bowl
He yearned to show his prowess
In destroying tinier things
Paul took rabbit from cat,
Betrayed, cat shrieked
They grow chickens now in cages
A life in in a cage
Poor rabbit.
Food for the already full.
Words to fragment pity
which do nothing to help no thing
Ineffectual affections
Caught in a steel trap
With a cat.

MORNING WINDOWS

How wrong to watch him while he's sleeping there
A death-head draped in red mouth opened so
Yet his warmth
touches mine in sleep
As I watch cold window vines across the room
The ivy spies to see if life's still there
After the tender battles of the night

Is love so violent or hate so tame
That hate's a crow to steal our better selves
Could moments when I am almost you
Be kindling to life's gluttonous flame?
Is warmth a bird of prey seeking carrion
As the sun feast on fresh slain meat

When I was small, I saw God in
Church windows
Living in one small glass all stained in blue
Now glass is clearly secular
A window spying love
And love's a part of hate
As clear is part of blue
Black night meets morning light
And all's gone grey.

CALYPO'S HOME IN GEORGIA

Tell me where you live and I will take you home
Home to gentle pine forests
Swaying softly in   the cool night air
Where the children speak slowly to each other
And the only loud noise is the train
Where the swamp hen builds her nest in the marsh
And the weather's never cruel, never harsh
Do you need a home?
You can come with me.
I've taken hurt things home before.
At first you might not like it
I won't let them throw you out.
They've gotten use to strangers
they will get use to us
Besides you've no other place to go.
You might not like the people and nothing turns out right
The air will smell like cabbage all the time.
But its someplace you can be from if you only would
And you can stay in one place for a while.
I can tell by looking that you need healing time
This city's tried to kill you and it will
Dogs die in the street and people in their cars
Death's not a part of life
"You say you want out here
Sure, I'll stop a while.
There's a little café up a mile
Hope you catch a ride now
Or build a raft
To where you want to go."
Sorry you're not coming home with me.
Hermes, Hermes,
 I have done what you asked.

OLEANDER DREAMS

Fangie pangies pink hour blooms now in Key West
In wasteful nature's green Oleander dreams
And while I sit in the North's naked winds
Beau Gregories swim in a   neon blue sea
 Rock Beauties call and tease a tropical me
Drilling in their black waters like Sargeant Majors
I shall meet you in those Oleander Dreams
Dressed in black to call out to the shore
Like a Queen Angel to a diver's eye
Calls him deeper with whiskered beauty,
Or a Jewel Fish to a poor mariner
Appearing as some costly Alexandrine,
French Angels can dart past cutlery coral
And the black weeds of urchin puffs
Rock Beauties can tease urchins
But it's a deadly affair meeting there.

THE OX FOOT

The black ox foot trod in the sea of the meadow
Less we lose sight of his garden-tale
Groves study to sail on right course
Among the rocks and quick sands of home.
Sleep, angry beauty, shall I come to thee
There is a garden in her face
Thou art not fair for all of me.

What then is love but morning
What is the death but the black ox foot
Whether men laugh or weep
Most of that we get in this sea of a world
Is a silent and long dark sleep.
Oblivion this morning rap with unholy fire
And showed his hour-glass to my eyes.
I sleep with that thought of thee.

GAINESVILLE, GEORGIA BURIAL

Ridiculous that it should really rain
For the extra dash of little black umbrellas
Burying the strangers' heads as we tried to meet
Shoes splashed in the mud
Making holes towards a large earthly pit
Where magic words provided the excuse
For throwing rotting meat into a ditch.
"We were to be kind to one another
Forgiving, even as God, for Christ's sake
Hath forgiven you."
The visit to the funeral home
With fans blowing, thrusting off
The smell of poor decaying flesh;
A cheap quadruple occupancy in the home…
Strangers made family in their deaths
Four coffins to a room;
Nothing to be done
But look and listen to them say
Those vile comforting words
That make you want to kill so they
Can take her place if it's so easy
So easy as the brain decomposes
In the midst of horrid roses
Too late symbols, cheap satin ribbons
In wired up cardboard vases,
Why waste the awful expense of good glass.
They put her in a pink formal dress
So that all laced up,
She looked her best
And the happy groans of grief have a certain relief,
Each angry mourner suggesting
This is mine alone!
Ah, to worship the dead when there is no one else

To eulogize;
So that relief can hide the constant fear
Of the one last week we loved:
Until we put her underground
We are not safe, we mourners for ourselves
For the family declares "I have suffered much."
Gullied tears echo the mud as we are soothed
By the joys of despair and an old time metaphor
As the elderly walk away: "I have outlived her"
And the younger umbrella hidden gasp:
"Duty can be put away at last."

WORDS WORTH

Some of the warmth of the nest of my birth
And some of the pains of my birth, I feel
In my movement towards death.
When the cold winter drives me towards the tunnel
I have some of the walls surrounding me
Before my birth – Now after
And that same cry to let me out
Combines with the desire to stay
Away from this cold red world.
Is all our constant quarrel is about
While we beat our feet and grumble in a room.

THE ICE CREAM TRUCK

From out of a holocaust carnival
The ice cream man rides through his street
Enters the tree-lined hollow
With his hurley-burly songs,
Like the bells clanging telling of
The dark pits between his teeth.
There is a hard nickel sound and sight
To the flaking white paint riding on his truck
The poor intrude into this part of town
Riding a honkey ice cream truck,
As children run to offer dimes
And maids watch carefully out of doors
And the little beggars count their beats
To the music of the ice cream truck.

T.V.'S TITILLATING AFFAIRS

Each day we meet a man so like our own
If he had never met our lack of generosity
If we had never domesticated
That wildness that we loved
Into a homey robe-and-slippers man
But woman is made to ritualize,
Gather together, self-victimize,
And turn each cerebral affair
Into a picture tube measuring stick,
A husband mirror,
To inspect teeth and coat and thoroughbred,
To watch his gate and check the hooves
And buy and sell at the right moment
In the right market, a social stall
Like little vermin dancing over meat
Where goods and buyers check their paces
And calculate one another's places.

Another man is but another husband
Another woman but another wife
At yet another point in time,
Perhaps another life;
Pitifully not of the flesh
But a desperate departure
From the grocery list present
Into a cartoon place and space
Where our little minds race
Where we hope to recall
A self long gone or never there at all,

Another five and ten cent self,
Lamented over breakfast dishes
Or the calming thrill of another pill
And the paranoid stare of the Frigidaire.
What maudlin moments precede our numbing
While we measure our   mate
And beg for the job of the heart's reawakening
Or ask for another plate
In some pornographic rebirth,
A little titillating guilt,
Where the only vision is television,
Revision or indecision,
A schizoid division…
Mrs. Jennings who plays bridge on Tuesdays
Calls
And the telephones tells, tells, tells.

THE PALINODE

A song of dejection and warning to the young
Cruel rejection
Of excited, unrequited ambition towards
One's betters
Poets, princes displaying tragic stances
In satire or romances;
Victims of their own positioned dances
Translators of a world our dizzy heads
Aspiring natures with our soaring love delusions
Reaching such overtiring conclusions...
I have been dejected in love of words
Birds, symbols of souls and sounds
Sleep laziness, plagues after honors
As I bemoan my loss and warn:
Why waste another day
Searching after the soft sharp wordy way
For in my mind my flocks will not feed,
My ewes breed not within my head,
No speeding rams echo my complaint
And in their ashes lives no faded fire.
Who am I to warn you from his little journey?
Between my mouth and ear

There is a sad affair.

DROWNING OFF MARSEILLE

You get a lot of water up your nose
In the baptismal font
It's no wonder the world prefers
Christening with little drops on baby heads
But drowning off Marseille
Even if you swim awhile,
In shorter, puppy strokes
out distance the rest in rough waters
Are mourned by ladies from Spain
Is still a shame and pain
Afloat for a moment next to our own boat
Envisioning the mahogany cabin
The velvet and the bar
It has gone too far.
Water all through the head
You retreat to the back
Of your eyeball, betrayed
Incanting over a blue speckle
Tasting the salt of the smoke house
Eyes gone out, distilled to juice
Into the smell of fish.

THE WINTER SOLSTICE

The ball of the year's evening has rounded
Rolled to a dark stop of dead black
Before the sun begs its coming back
And we warm ourselves with little spheres
Of cookies, cocoa, buttered rum
And open the closet to ascertain
That our seersucker and straw hat remain
For December is almost as dangerous
As February and July.
Winter's night makes purple talk
Together in a knee bent room
Hobbling their hands close to their face
Clutching the hot cocoa, or
Edging towards a kitchen hearth
Denied by the contractors
Of modern apartment ruins.

THE RETURN OF THE KNAVE

The court magician, the joker and the Prince
Began a game of cars in the gazebo
Where out of doors no courtier could stare
And evening softened Riga's shaded glare
As the musician fiddled with his underwear
For flesh and bones, rank beds and fleas
At the cars the jester would always sneeze
Whenever Prince was losing at a game
Begot of witches the magician fumed
Wished the jester an early tomb
The caged birds began to cry
As dragon flies buzzed over cakes and ale.
My peridot, my wallet and my gloves
Yeah, the seersucker of my pants leg too
Are gone. The prince deserted in a rash
Gently, gently cried the magician
The castle bard stopped talking in the halls
The palace guard arrived, the jesters called
Urchin-filled bushes giggle at the sight
Of princes sans sweaty jockey drawers
Are you waiting for the metaphors?
The king arrived and saw the dimpled knees
Prince de rigeur de factoese
The court magician looked at his colleagues
Withheld a smile and prayed
Then asked a page to spare
The king and bring an extra pair
Of prince's satin, laced underwear.

GRAVE-WATCHING

Sick chickens swept out from under the house
As Petunias fall over their lard can
too tired to stand up straight.
Rusting cars crowd the front yard
And all the porch rockers have reedless holes.
But time flows in the seasons
Holds itself like pansies in a tire
And there's never any reason
To check your watch or catch a train
Or go into Atlanta to explain
Why you're five minutes late
At doing something you don't want to do.
Hydrangeas are the only status symbol
Unless you can count
The paper fans the funeral home sends
Ticking like a country clock counting out
The sermon in the Southern Baptist Church.
Lilacs and Hollyhocks
For their strong old smell
Adorn the outhouse
While thrift was always planted on a hill
And grows there still as ferns around a well.
The most exciting thing to do
Is to go grave watching
To scare you and whoever you've bet
Was too afraid to go.
So you claim that hill which they say belongs
To no one, though it is always called
Allisonia
And crowd among the moss markers
Telling ghost stories
In hopes that you scare to death
The other guy

So you can leave
Before he knows you're chicken
And want to go so bad
That your heart's off on a run
Ten feet ahead of you toward home.
But you stay quiet and sit and watch your shoes
For though it's June
You'd never go barefoot
And let all that death seep into your feet
Like planter's warts.
Rays of fear wrap around you heart
As you laugh and wait
Til Sue Evans says
"I gotta get home;
It's getting late
And ma would whip me if she knew
that I was running over graves
Not knowing who I was walking on
And who was turning and all
And getting upset
And what bad luck it might have been
But I ain't scared, don't you think that

I just got things to do with my time.
There's homework I've put off."

And we went home to shelling beans
Flipping hem across the room.
But I've been grave-watching ever since
And many nights I walk that hill.

ESTRANGED

We partake of the nature of   what we oppose
In a dalliance we never allow
And our heart's store is almost closed
 Before we realize
We're all sold out.
We had hoped to fashion two noble persons
In a marriage that really was,
But I have come to understand a word
Estranged, making strangers,
Where once there were friends
And we must begin again
To know each other, like that first day,
A disappear splendidly dramatized
By using a gentle discipline
We begin again, once more,
For neither has ever really said
That all the feeling that we had was dead
And the numbing sensation of beginning again
Gives way to the smiles of an old, old friend,
Met again.

MEDUSA'S EYES

Gorgon pain remains the constant
Shame and pain those dogs running from a blow
Companions for the raw flim
Cheap self-disgust
Bruises turn one into pulp
To end somewhere the job too crase to be
The bone which aches and holds
The eyeball that can sometimes see.

L'ALLEGRO

When I have finally had enough
Of trees and books and flowered hills
And poetry just seems to be
A form of me speaking to me
Then I turn back to friends again
enjoy the laughter of smoke-filled rooms
And talk to my neighbor mowing his yard
Or eat my lunch with the folks at work
But in not too long I have had my say
And I go back to that same old way
Of feeling I said all that I am
And I'm no longer what I said
So I go back to books and barns
Or better yet, some North Georgia hill
And become what I said I am again
And the quiet of my mind, I till.

BLUEBIRDS: YOURS AND MINE

Some people say they can remember
When they were small, almost not at all
And they remember their first year
Almost as if it were still here
But I remember what I recall
First of all – an old jelly glass
That grandma washed the label off
And set up high in a cupboard place
And just as I remember that face
I can see three bluebirds race
Across the glass and I would ask
If I could use that glass for tea
If it could only belong to me
And when I see some chair, lamp or vase
Or Paul brings home a new thing for the house
Those three bluebirds appear again
In just another form
Since bought or paid for
I don't feel its mine
Until I go to look first in its place
And I recall my grandmother's face
As she assured me that small glass was mine.
If anyone can own blue birds.

A SMALL SISTER

Who is there to kiss away your tears
When the sunshine in our eyes through listening rain
Tiny smilettes play on your lips
There vanish with the grief remembered
Come with me and we will be
Streams of light, golden rain.
Little lady, I am bound to love
With the ties of laughing children's games
And the me that as a child
Proudly held my tiny doll
And many nights when I was grown
I held that children's plaything child
In the pain of knowing that all's been done
And I will never kiss away those tears again;
And the fear of never hearing, and no one being
Or ever seeing, those small tears again.

MY FATHER'S RUBBER TREADS

One way or another
It's myself, I address,
As I watch the windshield screen
Out the flattened cats, possums,   burst dogs
The low flying birds which thump against the car
And join the others marching on this road.
Hardened, I am prepared for a blur to be
Some headless wild thing as the car springs
Roaring ahead;
But the next corpse appears to me
Only a used up tread casted off
As the tire wheels swerve to avoid their dead comrade.
Another dead tread layers the road behind us.

THE RAG BAG

Too well, I know how in the
Long hours of the night
As my neck rebels the toil
Of holding up my heavy eyed head
I long to sleep a death-like sleep of rest
And close my eyes
As the soft sliding   lids shut mercifully
After the work of a too hard day.

Then I remember with what rested joy
I wake to find myself
Covered with patch worked comforters
Stitched together
Grandmother's woolen puzzle,
A hodgepodge she religiously made
At least one patch each day
In a work which never finished
And layered in bags and rags of scraps
Cut neatly, already shaped, fixed
In the bleary weary eyes
Of the old woman's workaday world.

OTHER ANAPHORA LITERARY PRESS TITLES

PLJ: Interviews with Best-Selling YA Writers
Editor: Anna Faktorovich

Inversed
By: Jason Holt

Notes on the Road to Now
By: Paul Bellerive

Devouring the Artist
By: Anthony Labriola

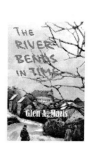

100 Years of the Federal Reserve
By: Marie Bussing-Burks

River Bends in Time
By: Glen A. Mazis

Interview with Larry Niven
Editor: Anna Faktorovich

An Adventurous Life
By: Robert Hauptman

CPSIA information can be obtained at www.ICGtesting.com
Printed in the USA
LVOW07s0930060914

402769LV00001B/32/P